Black
Women
Are
Dope!

BLACK WOMEN ARE DOPE!

A Poetic Anthology

Curated by: Stacy "Simply Stacy" Wilson

An Imprint of
Following His Way Publishing

Black Women Are Dope: A Poetic Anthology
Curated by Stacy Wilson (pen name: Simply Stacy)

Edited by Following His Way Publishing
Cover designed by Stacy Wilson

ISBN: 978-0-9887188-7-6
Printed in the United States of America.

For more information, visit:
www.mysisterssoulproductions.com/fhw
Instagram: @mysisterssoulproductions
Facebook: @MSSProds

LCCN: 2025922118

Contributing Authors:

Angella Kim-Mack (pen name: Southern Soul)

Danielle Savage (pen name: Elle)

Doneil Sauveur (pen name: BlackBird)

Kiera Nelson (pen name: Ashlee Haze)

Krishann McConico (pen name: Queen Floetry)

Krystal G. Williams-Murray

Patricia Monique Shaw, LSW (pen name: Miss Lady)

Shay Harrison (pen name: Suaveee)

SheRo Kennedy (pen name: SheRo Forever)

Sherry Clay (pen name: Sher the Poetess)

Stacy Wilson (pen name: Simply Stacy)

Tia Glenn-Scott (pen name: HigHER Power)

Treva Johnson (pen name: His Poet)

Wanesha V. Spencer

Yolanda Paige (pen name: Shining Poetess)

"Black Women, you are loved."

TABLE OF CONTENTS

Ashlee Haze

"If you want to be a good writer you should listen more than you speak and read more than you write. Then find the thing that still needs to be said."

hymn – Ashlee Haze

lean in,
let me tell you of a wall-less church
a congregation of women in the business of saving
women who do the heavy lifting while the world
gawks from the sidelines
women given the trash and the broken
and refused to think you disposable
women serving as a second womb
for the motherless
for grown men intent on not doing their own
emotional work
and we let you bask in our greatness
should you be so lucky to be granted the magic
because we might side eye you to kingdom come
might roll our eyes till you poof into oblivion
and ain't that sorcery?
the way our defenses protect us from elements
from a winter of the undeserving intent getting all of
our harvest

and you so vain think we do this for you
as if we wake up in the morning pandering to the
world's gaze
as if the aunties have nothing better to do than raise
kids that aren't theirs
as if the women of Atlanta and Wakanda had nothing
better to do other than to save men from themselves
lean in,

they saved themselves fist and you got saved in the
process
ain't that the way it goes?
we get dressed in all the work we do
and you are saved just by touching the hem of our
garments
black queer women create social justice movements
and you make it about the men
men oblivious of their own privilege
men who demand we be black first and women when
it suits them
our intersectionality is an inconvenient myth
mysogynoir be a weed that keeps growing back
no matter how many think pieces we spray on it

the trouble with being the savior, though
is people usually don't think we need saving
don't think we need gentleness
to my sister's, I vow to be more gentle with you
I vow to be gentle with myself
know that we are worthy of someone who helps with
the work
too long we have dined with people
serving food from our own gardens
on tables we bought and built

all that I have I owe to black women
I say glory to the women who thought I was worth
saving
glory to the women who think I'm enough
even when I fall short

I say I see you
you be visible
and you be worthy of all this praise

Blackbird

"There is no such thing as too much - all I have to do is be me, be a woman."

To Be a Black Woman – Blackbird

I've cried more than I've laughed this year.
Tears that met sadness before they met joy,
before they met Christ,
when He had already met me.
He met me as daughter.
Child.
Bride.
Woman.
My kin will know what it means to be woman,
to be Black,
to be Bride of Christ,
to be all-encompassing and everything He needs me
to be.
It's terrifyingly beautiful:
sacrifice.
You see, being Black and woman
is a feat.
It is an honor, a tribulation all wrapped up in one,
bearing fruit, multiplying, and moving as He sees fit,
abiding in the One who made it possible
to be, Strong. Black. Woman.

To be
more than I thought I could be,
more than they thought I could be taking up space,
because we must.
It makes sense why they want to be us.
From the tips of our heads

to the soles of our feet
dwells resilience, elegance, and confidence,
the Holy Spirit's resting place.
We are more than enough.
So those tears
are not just for me,
but for those who come after me,
cradled in the arms of Christ.
Their tears will meet Him first,
before meeting anything else.

Elle Savage

"For every joy there is a price to be paid" - Egyptian
Proverb

Frequency – Elle Savage

Saints, we are being called to vibrate,
At a more heavenly **frequency**.
Moving a little more **decently**, equally peacefully and
organically
Seated. He's coming on a cloud
One day you'll **see Em.**

So, I will walk in humility but not **fear.**
Sharp as a **snake** and Adequate in the **faith.**
Because I know that my that my God is **near.**

So, I put on spiritual authority
Maturity in **Christ**
Walking in abundance and shining in the **light**
Of understanding and **freedom.**

And it is for **freedom**
That Christ has set us **free**
To be **unique** and **complete**
And when you sit back and think
Hasn't He been sustaining
You and **me?**

But God if only my ways were more committed to
keeping Your **statutes!**
Daily renewing at your FEET so that my spirit be
active.

Getting rid of worldly **baggage**. increasing spiritual
practice. through Routines and **habits**.
But I produce no good thing apart from Him.
He makes it all **happen**.

So, I put my head down
Hands to the **dirt**. I get to **work**.
Bearing fruit.
It's Bitter**sweet.**
You see this fruit ain't always **fresh**
But if I keep my **feet** shod with the preparation of
peace
There's no comparison. No judgment.
Sis, this faith walk ain't no **contest**.

Therefore, I will be humble and **rest**. And study to say
less.
So that I can be free.

Have me out here smelling like jasmine blossoms,
patience and Joy in the Holy **Ghost**.
A sweet-smelling aroma
Be like: prayers of the Saints lifted up in golden **bowls**
Taking deep **breaths** and taking off **ego**.

For an incorruptible **flesh**.
Going where the land of milk and honey is at a free
flow.
Where the wind whispers PEACE.
Streets of gold give way to **release**.

Where the light never goes out and the throne shines
with crystal clarity.
Saints we are being called to vibrate,
At a more heavenly **frequency**.
Moving a little more **decently**, equally peacefully
Because organically **seated,** He's coming
On a cloud, one day we will all behold and **see.**

HigHER Power

"May your dopeness outweigh your doubt!"

Dear Black Women – HigHER Power

They tried their best to reduce us. Despite, we rose up fierce as the Phoenix, transcended limitations and emerged with newfound wisdom and power. They demonized our rituals, yet we still offered them healing salvation before ours with the peace of a blooming flower.

Dear Black Women,

There is profound poetry in your perseverance. Your divinity is not something to be sought but rather remembered and acknowledged within. You are truly remarkable.

Divinity and resilience course through your very blood.

We are undeniably cut from a different cloth, with souls intricately carved from centuries past.

You carry the wisdom and strength of your ancestors on your back and embody excellence in every stride you take.

Your shoulders, broad and strong, were built to bear both the tender weight of a baby and the heavy burden of a boulder. No matter your size, you are fierce, mighty, and capable.

Fearfully and wonderfully made, you possess an innate ability to lead and follow and maintain a home with unparalleled grace.

Black women have historically kept homes, even through some of the most challenging circumstances, including times when they could not even find a place to rest their own heads.

We walk with the whispers of women who tirelessly tended to individuals who refused to treat them with proper respect. I am, of course, referring to a period when we were dehumanized and labeled as property.

Yet even in captivity, we moved with inherent divinity, using beautifully decorated headwraps not only to protect the spiritual essence of our coif but also to preserve and honor our rich culture.

They unjustly called you cursed, yet they never once discriminated against the pure white gold streaming from your blackened nipples that nourished the bellies of babies you didn't even birth.

Your body, a sacred temple, has always been sought after, for it was understood that our DNA holds the very blueprint of civilizations. Every era, every chapter of human history, has been blessed through the Black woman's rapture.

Resilience is a natural quality deeply embedded within us. We possess an extraordinary ability to bounce back from hardships that were designed to break our spirit. We have survived every trial we have ever faced and stand firmly, praying in the devil's face.

That same unwavering resilience echoed across the vast cotton fields, which relentlessly picked back at our flesh and our bone, nearly breaking us—yet it was ultimately no match for our enduring strength. What did not kill us only served to make us undeniably stronger.

Life itself lies between your thighs; she, the Black woman, hath birthed the earth.

We are righteous, natural-born fighters, especially when it comes to fiercely defending our family. Our warrior spirit remains ever ready, knuckles up, prepared to fight. Sis, we embody the unwavering courage of Shirley Chisholm, with her chiseled resolve and the inherent courage in our voices, speaking scripture with the same grace and inspirational impact with which Sarah Jakes Roberts rejoices.

Black women are divine, refined, and incredibly beautiful. Our beauty is truly undefined, regal, and naturally captivating. We are magicians with blessed hands, capable of parting seas into scalps with fine-tooth combs. We palm-roll manes into luxurious locs and plant intricate cornrows. We weave sew-ins like exquisitely stitched garments—we are always artists.

We can miraculously transform a two-inch pixie cut into thirty-four-inch knotless branches that flow gracefully to waist lengths, often adorned with charms and cowrie shells—paying homage to a history where these shells were highly valued as currency. We continue to wear them as symbolic coins, recognizing our inherent richness. We are goddesses.

We apply charcoal accents with earth tones to accentuate our almond-shaped eyes—rouge and highlighter to polish the mountainous crests of our radiant, toned cheekbones. We line our lips with wine-stained tips and smile wide because we know who we are. We do not require foundation; our skin is firm and tight, smooth as shimmering golden silk in the sunlight. Our blackness shines so incredibly bright!

We are the true epitome of strength and the living definition of love. From sisterhood to motherhood, we have diligently built nations up. Though much was endured, our essential work remains undone.

The Black woman is love; she is community, mother, daughter, sister. She unapologetically takes up space. Her very presence commands attention without needing to utter a single word. Whether in the sanctity of the home or the gravity of the boardroom, the warmth of the kitchen or the vibrancy of the salon, at the bustling grocery store, the familiar corner store, or courtside cheering passionately for her squad, she is consistently a game-changer, the mover and the shaker, transforming all that she touches into something undeniably much greater.

With this Midas touch, who then fills her cup? Where does her remarkable resilience come from?

She finds unwavering strength in prayer and profound peace in the gentle sunrays piercing through her drapes, serving as a constant reminder of God's boundless grace. She steadfastly relies on faith, patiently waiting to exhale when life feels overwhelming. She still prevails, time and time again.

She bends as though she's boneless and may break in moments of darkness, yet she inevitably reshapes her pain into powerful purpose. Because when the sun rises, the house will rise with it. We sage and speak powerful affirmations over ourselves, our beloved babies, and babe, to manifest protection as they navigate their days.

We heal through the nourishing meals we prepare, and the words that we speak, so real, possess the power to cancel noise and fill the voids. We are joy. We are the warm embers burning brightly in our children's eyes, the clear reflection of love's unwavering warmth that cannot be denied.

We pour love when no one else does, to build you up;
that's affirmation.
We carefully oil scalps and season cast-iron pans;
that's preservation.
We kneel with bowed heads and clasped hands; that's
restoration.
With ritual, we heal ourselves; yes, that is salvation.
We raise families with or without a man; that's
acclimation.

Please do not misunderstand my words, for there is
truly nothing like a strong king sitting alongside his
queen on the throne, a devoted lover, a steadfast
provider, a protector of his family, the true head of
the home. May we love them, and may we raise our
sons to someday become such men.

Black woman, sister girl, queen, empress, we would
be profoundly lost without your essence. When God
created you, the entire earth was unequivocally
blessed. You are truly the dopest.

Love and Light,

Tia Glenn

His Poet

"Don't allow the pain of yesterday to steal the joy of today."

SIS – His Poet

Sis, I'm not gonna stand up here & tell you no lie.
Because somewhere down the line,
It don't matter if you fine like wine,
Somebody gonna make the time
To test you.
It could be an outright enemy or part of your crew.
It could be many, or it could be a few,
Spectators, talking about, "Now what she gon' do?"
You know, the ones that try to make you miss your
step,
Energy vampires trying to make you lose your pep.
Sometimes tears fall & that's OK, because remember,
even
Christ wept.
You belong to Jehovah Sabaoth, and He gon' always
intercept.
Sis, God has dispatched angels to encamp around
you.
There's nothing to fear.
This is your divine appointment; we are meant to be
here.
You are brilliant with purpose. It is evidently clear.
Don't be so nervous about change. God may be
aiming to
switch gear.
They may attempt to steal your greatness,
But they will not succeed.
Savages come to distract & don't hold the capacity to

water your seed.

Stay vigilant, the devil has a feast of lies, and he'll try to force-feed.
You lack nothing in this world; God has graced you with all you'll ever need.
Sis, I won't rhyme in riddles; there's no desire to misconstrue.
I'll not speak of roses red or Texas bonnets of blue.
I need to reiterate what I know to be true.
You've been on hold for too long; you're up next in the queue.
Sis, I won't try to sell
Not even one fairytale.
If you haven't already, come on out of that shell.
You need not be ashamed, honey, I have been the woman at the well.
I am mandated to speak words of great significance.
Regardless of the circumstances, your existence is no coincidence.
Be cautious of pride, but don't skimp on confidence.
Wisdom is the side effect when you seek God through obedience.
Sometimes, in this world, we might have to fight.
Whether it be arrow by day or terror by night.
For we walk by faith and not by sight.
If you battle in prayer, everything will be alright.
Sis, you are lovely in your own special way.
You can conquer any obstacle that life may display.

You are bursting with light, a natural array.

Hold on, I've just a few more words to say.
God… told me to minister to your spirit.
He told me to speak life so that your heart & soul
could hear it.
Your birthing season is NOW; you are no longer just
near it.
Thrive in the will of the Almighty, and don't you dare
fear it.
Let your actions and words be one and the same.
Walk in your destiny… this is not a game.
Stand at attention & listen, God is calling your name.
Your inheritance has arrived; time to stake the claim.
Sis, during those quiet moments with you and your
reflection,
Don't get caught up in the web of self-rejection.
If you occasionally stroll down that road, it's time to
change direction.
You got the hook-up, girl, it's a heavenly connection.
He gives you outstanding ideas, outside of the box.
Take care of your health. Be cognizant of your
thoughts.
Be kind to yourself, it's OK if you can't always
connect the dots.
Spiritual eyes open, 'cause Satan always got plots.
Sis, trust your discernment, and trust what you pray
for.
God is the companion who walks you through
designated doors.
Dive deep within… there is much to explore.

If you fall down, you won't stay there, girl! get up off that floor.

Because the authority is inside of you to consistently rise.

Your value is not based upon what lies between your thighs.

Don't tell everyone your good news—some folks lowkey despise.

Mind the company you keep and know when it's time for goodbyes.

Sis, you're strong, but take moments to be as delicate as lace.

As a woman, there will be times you'll need to be selfish about your space.

Be intimate with God, there's no shame in laying on your face.

Live intentional. You can easily match energy, but can you strive to match His grace?

Krystal G. Williams-Murray

"Blessed is she who has believed that the Lord would fulfill his promises to her!" Luke 1:45 NIV

He Silenced Them All – Krystal G. Williams-Murray

Can you hear that?
What, you ask?
The silence of the noise!
The sound of complete silence is…
Is healing to the body when you have come from
hearing so much.
They were all talking,
And everyone had so much to say
But he silenced them all.
He heard what you heard, and He even heard more.
He listened closely in on
Their whispering,
Their murmuring,
Their complaining,
Their laughing.
He knew all about the moments where you
And your torment became the topic of their
discussions.
And how many chose to go about sharing your news
Instead of the good news that He offered.
You heard the thoughts that they put forth and their
opinions.
Oh, how the assumptions came upon His ears as well.
And then, He silenced them all.
He heard when people would say, where is your
God?
Oh, I thought you were this great believer!
What sin have you done in the dark that has finally…
Finally, decided to come to the light?

But He silenced that too.
He heard how people thought you were doing too
much from the beginning
And, how they were able to forecast your end.
But the most amazing thing about all that He heard
from them
Is that while He was able to listen to them, He heard
your cries,
He heard your plea,
He heard you decree and declare His word to no end
He heard how the internal torture would play with
Your mind,
Your body,
Your soul, and
Your spirit!
He heard the wars that you would put forth as you
laid in the floor
In your prayer closet just knowing that something
had to break,
He heard how you would lay your head on your
pillow.
And call out the name of Jesus repeatedly
Because no matter what you were going through,
you know His name hold power.
He heard how you would battle with yourself and
say...
That I know.
That I know,
That I know,
That I know...

That God would not bring me this far and leave me
now!
I just know that He would not do that.
He heard when you would cry out in repentance
Just in case you might had done something wrong,
He heard how you would apologize repeatedly
And laid all your sins bare.
He heard it and, He silenced them all.
Then, one day, the God that was able to hear it all
Came to see about you.
He let you know that He heard
And made you fully aware that silence was to come.
The miraculous thing is, He did not silence them
By whispering in their ears to shut their mouths.
He silenced them by bringing you out.
He silenced them by lifting you up.
He silenced them by restoring onto you everything
that you had lost
He silenced them by making you over
He silenced them by making you better
He silenced them by giving you more than what you
had before they started talking.
He silenced them all
And He is not done yet.
But do not use this silence my young child to
become…
To become boastful or prideful.
God said, use this silence to teach them who I Am.
Use this silence to show them that I Am always there.
Use this silence to let them know I can bring them
through as well.

Use this silence to make them believe.
I silenced them to help you
But my plan was always to save them to.

Miss Lady

"You educate a man; you educate a man. You educate
a woman; you educate a generation."

Just US for US – Miss Lady

Filled with immeasurable heartbreak, broken heart
aches it's a shame it takes this level to get one's head
on straight but as they say, those are the breaks.

Work twice as hard, half the pay even less respect.
But inflation decides so you swallow your pride and
do what you need to do for that check.

The click clack of heels on floors as you meet cold
eyes that don't hesitate to remind that your kind
doesn't belong ignite the fire inside as you encourage
courage to keep you company as you work for the
company that wouldn't hesitate to throw you out on
the streets...

Freedom fighting isn't fighting if we're not uniting to
make it possible to survive this world when we're
surrounded by wolves.

Stop settling for crumbs falling from tables you are
not allowed to dine at but can serve the elite just fine
at.

Can't pull up a chair, I mean how dare...you...I mean

I swear some of us just stare and try not to drown in
despair.

Look, it's just US for us
We keep flipping coins and waiting for lady fortune
to smile on us when it comes to their justice.

Keep waiting for change and you'll keep getting left
in the dust.

Keep waiting for gains you'll join those who went
before their time paying the cost

Let's honor their memories with more than tears and
endless replays reminding us of their loss.

In the meantime, society paints a pretty picture
position pathetic prophets in places while perfectly
portioning plenty of pitiful privileges that should be
rights.

And even for those — we have to protest, work twice
as hard, and fight.

Keep telling me it's not unreasonable for me to tell
my daughter the same thing that was taught to me —
passed down from generation to generation along the
family trees.

Some of which strange fruit blended with

Two strikes baby girl

Uno — Black

Dos — Female

Tell me truthfully, how many ethnic groups have to have a sit-down conversation and ruthlessly discuss the limitations that accompany racism, so they are prepared for the society they live in?

Keep telling me it's reasonable for certain people to have to be overqualified in order to be considered qualified. And how is it an equal opportunity when we have to have twice as much and work twice as hard for what is supposedly equality?

Mic check 1, 2, 3.

For so long we've been frequently fed fanatical lies can it really be considered a surprise when some crack under the pressure and believe the hypnotic hype?

Do you believe in magic

No.

Gotta work twice as hard, half the pay, and sometimes for even less respect.

If we think this is living, the concept is twisted, and the definition must be revisited because no one should be expected to live like this.

But let's stop complaining and find a fix.

Queen Floetry

"Then Jesus spoke to them again, saying, "I am the light of the world. He who follows Me shall not walk in darkness but have the light of life." **John 8:12 NKJV**

Taking Their Innocence – Queen Floetry

What am I supposed to do
when ICE and twelve are chasing you?
And what am I supposed to say,
when parents are locked up and you're not okay?
I'm fallin' to pieces, yeah...

On the last day of school,
when children are supposed to laugh and play,
I'm consoling my kids
on the most somber day. See...

One of my girls lost her mom that day,
ICE came to her job and took her away.
Now she and her siblings have to cross the border.
Any day now, the life she once knew is over.

And I... feel conflicted.
"Told you so" sticks to my lips for the 54%,
while my heart aches at losing kids
I just taught about decimals and earthquakes.

They said when the heart breaks,
it don't break even,
because there's no fraction that can piece together
the fractures of losing my children.

And since the Neanderthal descendants
want racial division with subs they can track,

not knowing they're causing discontinuity,
because there is no amount of hatred
that will fill the hole of their inferiority.

They attack those who bring value
and vitality to jobs they won't even do,
because us Blacks are statistically higher educated
and know how to make a dollar out of fifteen cents,
while your meemaw's working at Walmart
because she voted for the man
who took away the welfare assistance
that helps her pay her rent.

While the adult's bicker
about whose ideologies are right,
my kids, the ones I taught to dream big
and become leaders,
are having nightmares
about being snatched tonight.

Now, what am I supposed to say
when my kids don't come to school
fearing they'll be taken away?
And what am I supposed to do
when I can't protect them
from the monstrosities of the red, white, and blue?

I'm fallin' to pieces... yeah.

Sher the Poetess

"Never Settle."

I Am Not the Baby Momma; I Am My Son's Mother
– Sher the Poetess

The only regret and mistake made is who I was
involved with.
Out of that mistake, God gave me my greatest gift.
I am not the baby momma; I am my son's Mother.

I chose to carry my son when asked not to, so I knew I
wouldn't be supported.
But asking for his support, I never had to, God has
been very devoted.
I am not the baby momma; I am my son's Mother.

The manipulation and games continue even though I
refuse to participate.
My biggest concern is not for me but my son, and
how he will navigate.
I am not the baby momma; I am my son's Mother.

Social media people support false narratives; he
paints pictures without absence.
When the reality is there might as well be an obituary
and a closed casket.
I am not the baby momma; I am my son's Mother.

The tears I cry are not in vain, though it feels like it
because of continuous pain.
I am still grateful, for my son is sunshine in this
never-ending rain.

I am not the baby momma; I am my son's Mother.

SHERO

"Those who live right never die. The seeds of their memories will germinate in the hearts of the ones they've touched."

DOPE – SheRo Forever

There's thunder beneath your feet when you step in
the room.
A reverberation so undeniably powerful, it's visceral.
Even unaware, you own the space.
So, let this be the last time you need to be reminded to
'own' your space.
You are dope.

Dope, like brilliance too sharp to dull.
Like a heart strong enough to cradle despair and still
make room for joy.
You are dope.

Dope like Harriet Tubman, Ida B. Wells, and Shirley
Chisholm.
The very dopeness that continues to permeate history
The kind so masterfully mirrored through Jasmine
Crockett, Ketanji Brown Jackson, and Sheila Jackson
Lee.
Their courage is the current flowing in me, in you, in
us.

Sis, we come from memory keepers, grandmothers
who hummed freedom into soul food, aunties whose
side-eye held the power to reset the room, sisters who
showed us how to wear our skin like armor.
Mothers who raised nations despite being told they
were "too much."

We are the blueprint and the remix,
the dream and the manifestation.

We've built empires out of whispers.
Organized revolutions in between clock-ins and
clock-outs, stretched paychecks into miracles,
and still showed up polished, smiling, unbroken.
We survived what was meant to undo us.
Dopeness is not what we wear.

It's what we ARE.
And if you ever forget, let this remind you:
you are incredible, undeniable, irreplaceable.
From one dope chick in Blackness to another,
never doubt it.

Shining Poetess

"Life is not about waiting on the storm to pass. It's about learning to dance in the rain."

Black Women are Indeed, DOPE. – Shining Poetess

Black queen...
Get closer with that lyric lean…
To the…scene the poetess bout ta set…
Black women have got to be the dopest creation yet.
We come in all shapes and sizes…
Layers on luscious with hair the kinda kinky that only
God could've notarized…
And…
Skin dipped in shades that they stay tanning trying to
match that
meldin...melodious melanin
Piling on the potatoes or padding to pull off these
hips while shooting botox in
their lips…
Throwing on wigs to rock our fros and locs...
Spin the block...
You can't duplicate an original.
The tools needed to create a black woman's majesty....
has to be supernatural...
Dig this truth y'all….
Black woman, you were consecrated for greatness,
baby!
Shaped and molded, crafted and chosen... from the
bronze curvaceous spheres to
the mocha folds...
God made that, chiseled that, straight bedazzled,
she's just that cold.
A beauty to behold...

So powerful in her innovation,
Nothing but the deepest of connotations.
Alluring and evocative in her gaze.

Intellect engineered to lift and shift the haze...
Til it's blue...
The Potter fashioned her to bless you no matter what
it do...
She can....
Call down destinies while multiplying the vision.
Don't sleep on this wonderfully made vessel of
wisdom.
Plot twist, son.
Here's the gist...thanks to the One!
Our beauty hits the whole BEHOLD DOPENESS
list...It keeps going and going...
You out your rabbit mind if you don't understand we
are the very definition of
God's rose dipped in DIVINE!
Strength embodied like mountains that stand tall
above everything you throw at
her! Infinite possibilities roaming the peaks of these
pieces locked in perpetuity.
Copernicus couldn't even do the math....
Formulate an understanding of all the hype...
It's the prowess behind our might...our flight and our
insight,
She can never be tamed, won't eva be ashamed...with
a shine that glows and
grows, unapologetically a force...and the world and
its substitutions stay tryin' dull

our light.
And it's time for us beautiful melanated queens to
illuminate beyond the hate!
It be facts whether Ripley believes it or not!
Open your eyes!!
recognize the jewel you got in your presence…
Allow me to reintroduce myself…
I'm a diamond mine.
So, you can call…me the shine…

Or refer to me as the great black hope…
Because God made me and every black queen…
Just…that…dope.

Southern Soul

"What's keeping you hidden isn't humility... It's fear.
God called you to be seen.
Rise up, Woman of God.
You've been called to build bold."

If Love Was a Weapon – Southern Soul

If love was a weapon,
she'd be a Black woman.
Lips loaded with hymns and war cries.
Hips swaying with the balance of heaven and hell.
Voice slick with sermons and side-eyes.
A triggered tongue that could birth kingdoms
or burn down bridges with a whisper.

She's not made of steel.
She is steel.
Forged in fire and fried fish Fridays,
seasoned with scriptures and sass.
Her silence is more dangerous than any man-made
missile.
She doesn't need a safety on.
She is the safety.
The "come home" after chaos.
The "don't make me come down there!"
The prayer whispered between gunshots and
paychecks.

She carries revolution in her ribcage,
grandma's grit tucked behind molars,
mama's mourning's stitched into her Sunday best,
and a whole bloodline of women who made miracles
outta "make do."
She's the reason "still standing" ain't just a phrase,
it's a flex, and not just a testimony.

Call her loaded,
not just with pain but with praise,
with poems passed down like pocketknives
and prayers wrapped in lace.
Every bruise is a blueprint.
Every scar is a sacred scripture
etched in melanin and memory.

You see,
she doesn't need reloading.
She rebirths,
shoots truth from hip,
healing from holler.
God didn't just make her,
He molded her from thunder,
lined her spine with psalms,
and crowned her with don't try me.

He did His thing when He made her.
He didn't hold back,
Not a single drop of divinity.
She's not just love.
She's the battlefield and the blessing,
because you don't survive centuries of war
and still love this loud unless you're the weapon
and the reason the war ever ended.

So next time you see her,
don't flinch.
Stand firm in her presence and understand:
you're not just looking at a woman.

You're witnessing what happens when God makes love lethal and calls her a Black Queen.

SUAVEEE

"There is no greater agony than bearing an untold story inside of you."

Biblical Journey - Suaveee

I had been cursed since birth,
Like Genesis, this is only the beginning.
When she touched me, just like Cain and Abel, she
was able to bury me way deeper than just
the surface.

I felt like I died that day.
Was marked with lies, lost the gleam in my eyes.
How could you imagine something so ugly
to appear more beautiful?
The serpent swallowed up God's law and purpose.
Cunning but never wise, he will always be one's
servant, slithering, sliding, looking for greater
service. A different place to hide.
Opening windows and doors to the darkest places
where secrets begin to lie.
A misleading fortune, not even zodiacs can show the
signs.
Swallowing more than just the serpent's pride,
Captivity setting me up to die,
Pacifying me with a lie,
passing over the Word that would inevitably help me
to survive.

As the serpent passes through, leaving me without a
clue, 'cause that's what stalking innocent
prey would do.
Surrounding and feasting,

ambition on seeking, intensely showing
The proof of when the serpent starts devouring you.
I touched the shrine, where curses lie,
In deep fear of being left behind. For those who don't
believe me, this is what being self-
righteous will do.

Boldly, yet slowly, the serpent began to feast on my
underdeveloped mind. Failing to nurture,
Learning secrets can cause a divide.
Due to my rhyming,
In less-than-perfect timing,
a numbers game began to muster up a prideful rage.
The serpent began to claim his stay.
An identity change,
caused a great delay, because I forgot how to be
courageous and brave,
To hold on to the promise in Joshua, where the Truth
still remains.

As the serpent prepares to hold feast,
I presumed my defeat,
Then asked God to console me.
Those demons get controlling,
In possession, withholding truth so boldly.
Then truth came in, warring with a Judge Whose
Sword was scolding.
The serpent simultaneously started recoiling,
retreating without me knowing.
This Prophetess would prepare me for new life from
the one I had been destroying.

Now I've been told,
"I'm not good for nothing," but following famine and
death took away all the doubt in me.
So proudly, I stand like Ruth for all the ones who
doubted me.
I got a new praise and shout, because the serpent has
been moved out of me.
With humility and grace, my training takes place.
Now I'm proud to see the books that's in store from
proclaiming patience to a nation.
That I am a training Prophetess, named Shay Lyn
Harrison, a new-named gift.
The rebuilding restored.
Repurposing my purpose I once called destroyed.

Distinguishing the establishment, prominent polish
for the crown God placed me in,
To lead some minds to freedom where bondage
quietly keeps them in.
'Cause the only way to freedom is to know God's
faithful, no matter how bad suffrage is.

Wanesha V. Spencer

"I believe one of the most profound things you can do
is forgive yourself."

"Dear Sir..." – Wanesha V. Spencer

I dedicate my poem "Dear Sir" to the amazing Father Figures God placed in my life.
Your presence is connected to my evolution as a woman. Thank you..

My Loving Grandfather - Walter J. Spencer
My Chosen Father - John Brown
My Godfather - Dr. Cody L. "Spec" Clark
My Favorite Uncle - The late Emory Howard

This is an open letter to Fathers Figures everywhere

You.. are appreciated
For being who you are and owning your position
Despite any disposition or circumstance
You took a chance at loving someone else

A modern-day Joseph in the physical
A representation of a seed..
Weather biologically or spiritually
You're a hero in our eyes

Not because you're perfect
Or never made a mistake
You wear that imaginary cape
Without the fanfare

Ain't no camera crews or reporters documenting your
day
Yet you show up in ways only a man can
You understood the assignment
Taught me how to square my shoulders

Look folks in the eyes when I'm talking

Taught me it was safe to depend on you
Lighten my defenses
Trust in someone other than myself

Encouraged me to be strong
Yet acknowledge when I need help..
You were my first teacher, mechanic, and comedian
Took my own mental notes when you thought I
wasn't listening

I always watched you when you didn't notice
I saw strength in your perseverance
Hope in your determination
Wisdom in your silence and love in your actions

Yet.. to some
This poem might not make any sense
But it represents every man with or without children
Who decided to answer the call

Granddads,
Uncles,
Step dads,
Teachers,
Coaches,
And, mentors
Who said yes when duty called
I honor you…

For every single solitary sacrifice

For every conversation
For your time
For your effort
For your attentiveness
And, for your love

For it mirrors the heart of my Heavenly Father

The Blueprint
The Epitome
Of Love

Simply Stacy

"Now to Him Who is able to keep you from stumbling and to present you faultless before the Presence of His Glory with Exceeding Joy." **Jude 1:24 NKJV**

Seasoned Saints & Sunday Plates – Simply Stacy
(Homage to 927 Wills Road)

Sundays smelled like salvation.
Greens simmered in smoked turkey testimonies,
fried chicken anointed in hot grease and glory,
macaroni so cheesy it could lay hands.

The saints wore white,
but the food?
The food was colored in deliverance
golden cornbread, red Kool-Aid, banana pudding
kissed by angels.

Big Mama, never read from cookbooks.
She read from memory, from the Holy Spirit,
from passed down prayers whispered over cast-iron
pots.
"Lord, let this food nourish our bodies."
And somehow, it always fed our souls more.

We didn't eat fast.
We dined slow.
Savoring stories, passing grace, testifying between
bites.

Cousins argued over the last deviled egg,
but quieted when Granddaddy prayed.
He'd say, "God, thank You for provision,"
and we'd hum our amens with full mouths
and even fuller hearts.

This wasn't just dinner.
It was communion.
A table where everyone had a seat,
where laughter echoed louder than lack.
Where sorrow didn't get the last word
Joy was baked into sweet potato pies.

The food was her ministry.
That kitchen, her sanctuary.
And every Sunday,
the Gospel showed up
like gravy.

The Woman in the Thread
(for my mother)

She stitched joy into my days,
Her hands danced like tambourines
over fabric and flour,
gathering glory in the folds of a hem,
in the rise of a pound cake,
in the scent of something simmered slow.

Her fingers were gentle.
Nothing loud about them, steady.
With every thread of a needle,
She hummed hallelujah.
In every seam, a praise.
She baptized linens in suds and prayer,
ironed out wrinkles the world tried to press in.

She called everyone, "dear."
And carried a smile that could hush a storm.
Kindness hung on her like perfume, and somehow,
she made this girl with the different walk
feel like royalty,
her dark-skinned daughter,
feel like the sun.

I watched her wrestle
with sorrow in silence,
shadows that clung like old coats
but even then,
she wore hope like her best dress

and lit candles in cracked places.
God met her somewhere between the stove and the
sewing machine.

And I, a wide-eyed girl
had a front-row seat to Grace,
learned that being a woman
meant feeding the world
while fasting your own grief.
It meant praying with raw hands
and loving without proof.

She is gone now but not gone.
She lingers in lace curtains,
in "dear's spoken soft,
in hymns hummed over sinks, in every thread of me
that refuses to break.

When you speak of
Black women who endure,
who create, who rise,
know that she walked among them.

My Daughters Make Art of Themselves
(the artists I birthed)

I have watched galaxies gather at the fingertips of
girls I named.
Watched paint turn to praise and pliés birth prayers
in rooms where silence once sat.

One bends color like it owes her joy,
threads copper and charcoal into the soft belly of
canvas, layers memory into form, The Holy Spirit into
shadow, teaching torn paper how to bloom.
The world pays attention because it knows
when it is being seen for real.

The other lives in the music her body makes.
Each leap a legacy. Each turn, testimony.
Classically trained, yes,
but she carries innate talent in her ribs,
a rhythm only the free can feel.
She pirouettes through pain and lands soft in praise,
a whole sermon held in her spine.

They both make miracles with their hands, their feet,
their minds, taught me that art isn't just what you
make, it's who you are becoming while making it.

I didn't just raise daughters.
I raised movements. Brushstroke and ballet. Ink and
intention.

Their lives are layered in Holy expression,
and I thank God for letting me be the first gallery
they ever walked into.

This is Dedicated To...

Simply Stacy

To my Lord and Savior, Jesus Christ, thank You for the gift of poetry and the spoken word. Had it not been for the Words You spoke none of this would be. Thank You for the opportunity and privilege to connect souls together to bring You Glory by way of artistry. It never feels like labor, just an offering of Love when You allow me the opportunity to sow into the earth creatively.

To my fave 4: Jelani, Terrell, Sydney and Joi, thank you for being my biggest cheering section and for always making sure I do whatever The Lord calls me to do. You never let me wade in the pool of my insecurities and for that I say thank you, thanks for holding up my arms when I've grown weary.

Lastly, to the ladies who've partnered with me on this project, THANK YOU for sowing your gifts, talents and creative anointing to this body of work. It is my hope that it encourages and empowers the hearts of the women who read it and as you read the pieces shared by other contributors that you too are inspired, empowered and encouraged to keep doing what you've been created to do. This book would not be with you! Thank you!

Blackbird
For the women before and after me - may my tears testify to His love and faithfulness.

HigHER Power
Mrs. Stacy Poellnitz-Wilson,

Thank you for every opportunity you have created for me to shine my light.

You made space for me even when I didn't know what to say, and you have continued to encourage me, uplift me, and pour into my soul.

Thank you for believing in me when I was still learning to believe in myself.

I am sending you the biggest thank-you and an air hug full of love. I am forever grateful that God allowed our paths to cross.

I love you dearly.

Thank you.

His Poet

I want to dedicate this to my mother. A woman who showed me how to be a woman, a woman who taught me strength, resilience, humility, and love. A woman who taught me in her own way how to be real, true and transparent. I am grateful for everything that she taught me and I'm grateful to God For making her my mother.

Miss Lady

I dedicate this poem to my daughter, Essence — my heart, my joy, my world.

Krystal Murray

To My Heavenly Father,

I just want to say, thank You! I want to thank You for coming to see about me when I needed You the most. However, You didn't just come to see about me, You pulled me out, made me over, and put me back on my feet with the understanding of who I am in and through You.

What a mighty God I serve! You deserve all the praise!

Queen Floetry

I dedicate this poem to my babies who are forced to live with adult mistakes. Ms. McConico loves you no matter where you are.

Sher the Poetess

This poem is dedicated to the first single mother I ever knew, my sister, Sharlotte Clay-Windmon. Thank you for leaving me the blueprint, big sis. I'm so thankful you got a chance to see me become a mother before you left this earth. Thank you for telling me how great of a mother I am; I promise to always strive to maintain that.

To every other single mother in this world, your extraordinary courage, perseverance, and never-ending love do not go unnoticed. You nurture and provide for your children, often while facing your own significant challenges, stress, and self-sacrifice. We are in this together.

SheRo

I want to thank God for putting the words in my heart to be able to articulate myself the way I wanted in this piece. I'm grateful for the life lessons that allowed me to be able to blossom into the woman that I am. I'm honored to share this body of work with other amazing women.

To Stacy: I would like to thank [YOU] for embodying everything you wanted this project to be. From the day I met you, you've been a light. You're the woman who everyone can meet one time and say, "I know God lives within her." I'm so blessed to know you and no matter how long we go without speaking to each other, we always pick up as though we never skipped a beat. You can't find that type of friendship just anywhere. You're beautiful, loving, encouraging, and God-fearing. My life is better with you in it my friend.

Shining Poetess
I dedicate this piece to Kaylah, my daughter, who is one of the dopest young ladies I know...and Vincent, my husband, who celebrates me out loud as the dopest black woman in his world.

Southern Soul
To every Black woman who has ever been underestimated yet still chose to love fiercely: this poem is yours. Thank you for carrying generations on your back and still finding room for tenderness.

And to every reader who found a piece of themselves in these lines, your presence here means everything. May these words remind you that love, in the hands of a Black woman, has always been more than soft; it's powerful enough to protect, to heal, and to change the world.

Suaveee
This poem is dedicated to the journey of becoming me. I'd like to dedicate it to my mom, Shelia Kincaid-Davis; my dad, James Harrison; my bonus dad, Audie Davis; and my spiritual mom, Jaycee Bradley.

A special thank you to those who have been manna unto me since day one — whether you're from Covenant U.C.C., St. Helena, Dirksen, Thornwood, H.F., Eureka College, Legacy Outreach Corp., the poetry community, or any of my jobs — you have all, in some way, inspired my Old Testament to get to the new.

Thank you for showing me why those three Es are important… it's because *you* are important!

Wanesha V. Spencer
My Foundation: First and foremost, I thank God. Apart from Him, I am nothing.

With Him, my life has meaning. To My Father Figures, please accept my poem, "Dear Sir" as a heartfelt thank you. My evolution as a woman is connected to your presence in my life. I am forever grateful. To my Mom, you are strength personified. It is an absolute honor to be your daughter. I love you with all my heart. I would also like to give a special acknowledgement to my grandparents, the late Walter & Ella Spencer. With God as the foundation, we navigated the journey together. Thank you both for raising me like one of your own. Your love continues to carry me. My angels, I am forever grateful.

Stacy: My dear sister "thank you" is a complete understatement. You are the blueprint and walking definition of true friendship and sisterhood. You are the embodiment of Black Women Are Dope: The Anthology. Thank you for creating safe spaces to uplift and encourage women and men. It is an honor to share this experience with so many amazingly gifted poets, writers, and storytellers. I speak blessings and continued favor over your life today, tomorrow and forever more. May God continue to bless your path while enlarging your territory. I love you, my sister.

Connect With the Authors

Ashlee Haze
Website: www.ashleehaze.com
Instagram: @ashleehaze
TikTok: @ashleehaze
YouTube: Ashlee Haze
Purchase & Stream Works: Ashlee Haze

Blackbird
Instagram: @poeticblackbird

Elle
Linktree: @Danielle Savage

HigHER Power
Instagram: @higherpower10

His Poet
Facebook: @HisPoet10
Instagram: @hispoet._/

Miss Lady
Instagram: @its_miss_lady/

Queen Floetry
Linktree: @queenfloetry
Instagram: @queenfloetry

Sher the Poetess
TikTok: @sherthemoments

Shining Poetess
Facebook: @blacklovepoetrytv
Instagram: @shiningpoetess

Southern Soul
Instagram: https://www.instagram.com/love_nlyrics/

Suaveee
Instagram: https://www.instagram.com/iam_suaveee/
Facebook: https://www.facebook.com/shayisSuaveee

Wanesha V. Spencer
Website: www.ellaproject.org
Instagram: @wanesha_spencer
Facebook: @wvs.poet
Purchase & Stream Works: Wanesha V. Spencer

www.ingramcontent.com/pod-product-compliance
Lightning Source LLC
Chambersburg PA
CBHW031858170626
46807CB00004B/1795